ZENISMS

DEDICATION For my teachers.

(Now look what you made me do.)

ZEN|SMS
LAUGHTER ON THE PATH TO ENLIGHTENMENT

DAVID BELL

Lothian
BOOKS

Thomas C. Lothian Pty Ltd
132 Albert Road, South Melbourne,
Victoria 3205
www.lothian.com.au

Copyright © David Bell 2002
First published 2002

All rights reserved. No part of this publication may be reproduced,
stored in a retrieval system or transmitted in any form by any means
without the prior permission of the copyright owner.
Enquiries should be made to the publisher.

National Library of Australia
Cataloguing-in-Publication data:

Bell, David, 1965 Dec. 2–.
Zenisms: laughter on the path to enlightenment.

ISBN 0 7344 0450 6.

1. Enlightenment (Zen Buddhism). I. Title.
294.3442

Designed by Lynn Twelftree
Back cover photograph by Bec Matthews
Printed in Australia by Pyrenees Press

INTRODUCTION

The stories, saying and anecdotes in this little book are inspired by teachings from the old Zen masters, as spoken to me by my own teachers. Many of these thoughts can be attributed in their essence to such great teachers as Dogen, Hakuin, Basho, Leo Tze, Yun-Men, Ikkyu, Ryokan and many others. It is a testimony to these masters that their ideas survive today and are still recounted in Dojos and Zendos across the world. ⟶ Classic sayings, such as, 'what is the sound of one hand clapping' and 'what is the difference between a duck', are adaptations of profound lessons, given as questions to students by their masters, with the intention that no logical thought would provide an answer. These questions, known as *koans*, allow us to think outside our usual intellectual process, and provide a space for insights into our own nature.

Some of the stories I have chosen will be familiar to many readers, as they have become a trusted way of relating the timeless wisdom of Zen and zen-like thinking. These parables give us an amusing glimpse into what it is to be human. ◂— There is a delightful playfulness in many of the old Zen teachings. At times, the masters would show irreverence to the concept that studying Zen was a sacred path *in itself*, reminding us instead that what we think of as ordinary *is sacred*, and that the path to enlightenment is walked by living wholly in this moment. ◂— *Zenisms* doesn't pretend to be a serious, profound book for the spiritual seeker, but it is the only book I know that reveals the secret to happiness in three words! ◂— Have fun.

This book has not been tested on dogmas.

Zen is the study of your true nature, by removing conceptual abstraction and attachment to illusion. This allows you to enjoy your porridge in the morning.

There is no point looking south

if your thoughts are in the north.

The future just arrived,

met briefly with the past

and gave us a little present.

A young monk walked up and down the bank of a wide, swiftly flowing river trying to decide how to cross it. Soon he noticed a person on the other side of the river who was a great Zen master. Thinking his troubles were solved he cried out to the wise master, 'Great Teacher, how shall I get to the other side of this river?' ▬◄ The master called back, 'You are already on the other side of the river.'

I'VE BEEN THINKING A LOT LATELY

AND I DON'T RECOMMEND IT

ZEN MEDITATION

Focus on the breath and clear the mind

of all thoughts, including this one.

A spiritual practice has no mind to gain merit,

but don't worry if it makes you happy.

For it has no mind to make you miserable either.

Lift your hand,

knock softly on the night sky.

Listen.

Not to do

is to do.

One day a venerable Zen monk and his student were walking along a path. The student stopped to pick up a snail. The venerable monk asked his student, 'What are you doing with that snail?'

'I was afraid we might step on it, so I am moving it from our path,' the student replied.

'But surely the snail was supposed to be here, at this precise place, at this very moment. Haven't you interfered with its karmic destiny?' the monk asked.

The student thought for a minute, then placed the snail back on the path.

'You are doing it again,' exclaimed the monk.

(The French version of this story varies slightly.)

Zen is not a sign

that points to a place

beyond itself.

A peasant farmer's much-prized horse ran away, and his neighbours cried, 'Oh, what terrible luck!'

'Maybe, maybe not,' the farmer said.

A week later the horse returned, bringing with it ten wild horses. 'What good luck,' the neighbours said.

'Maybe, maybe not,' the farmer replied.

While training the horses, the farmer's only son was kicked in the knee and crippled. 'What dreadful luck,' the neighbours said.

'Maybe, maybe not,' the farmer replied.

A week later an army came through the district recruiting soldiers. The farmer's son was spared because of his injured knee. The neighbours, who all lost their sons to the army, said,

'How fortunate you are!'

'Maybe, maybe not,' the farmer replied.

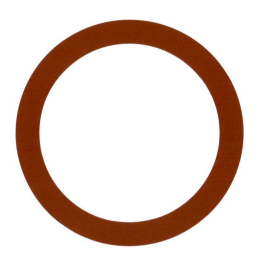

Is this upside down?

Anyone who laughs at their own foolishness has a constantly updated source of amusement.

I haven't seen any proof

of tomorrow all day.

NOW

seems as good a time as any.

Hot tea,

soft bed,

what more?

There was a venerable Zen master whose monks were in awe of him, because of his almost unworldly calm. To see if their master could be unsettled, the monks hid themselves in a dark hallway of the monastery and waited for the master to walk by. ⟶ When the master came gliding along the hall carrying a hot cup of tea, the monks leapt from their place of hiding and screamed at the top of their lungs. But the master continued along the hall peacefully. He entered his room, gently placed his cup of tea on the table, sat down in a chair and let out an ear-splitting cry, 'Ooaaah!'

The line between *thing* and

no thing won't keep still.

Zen cow explaining the concept of no-thing (*mu*).

Desiring enlightenment is like fighting for peace.

TO BELIEVE
YOU ARE HUMBLE

IS TO KNOW
YOU'RE NOT

'Can I ask a question?'

'Please ask your question.'

'I did.'

'I answered.'

'What was your answer?'

'Is this a new question?'

Nothing matters.

It really does!

There was a Zen monastery in which the monks lived a life of complete silence. There was one exception to this rule, each monk was permitted to speak just two words every five years. Having remained silent for five years, the abbot asked one of the monks to say his two words.

'Room cold,' the monk said.

Five years later the same monk was permitted to speak again.

'Food revolting,' the monk said.

Another five years passed and again the abbot asked the monk which two words he would speak.

'I'm leaving,' the monk said.

'I am not surprised!' the abbot replied. 'All we ever hear from you are complaints!'

Before enlightenment:

cooking dinner, washing dishes.

After enlightenment:

cooking dinner, washing dishes.

ZEN HEALTH PAGE

Zenophobia: the fear of sudden changes in your perception of reality.

Zenitus: ringing in the ears caused by over enthusiastic bell-gonger.

Zenpes: bunions on the nether regions after excessive sitting-meditation.

Zenaritus: really sore knees.

Zen drinking game: drink when thirsty.

LIFE DIRECTION

The West says, 'understand and transform yourself.'

The East whispers, 'know and transcend the self.'

The North and South are staying very quiet.

What is the sound of one hand clapping?

What was the other hand doing?

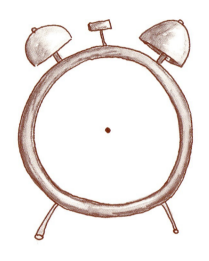

Zen o'clock

Only this is a fact: it will pass.

Only this is constant: change.

Only this exists: this moment.

A centipede crept along the path, his legs flowing in perfect synchronicity. ⏤ A toad marvelled at the centipede's progress and asked, 'How can you co-ordinate so many legs? Which leg must you move first?' ⏤ The centipede stopped to think about the question and is still trying to remember how to walk.

Asserting the name is hiding the nature.

An eager student of Zen asked his master how long it would take to truly understand zazen meditation.

'At least ten years,' the master said.

'What if I study twice as diligently?' the student asked.

'At least twenty years!' the master replied.

ZEN JOIN THE DOTS GAME

●

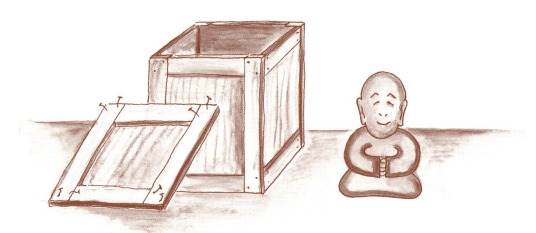

The Buddha statue

has as much Buddha Nature

as the box it came in.

Do I breathe the air,

or does it breathe me?

A Zen master and his student sat down to watch birds alight on the branches of a nearby tree.

'See how the birds delight in the tree!' the master said.

'You are not a bird,' the student replied. 'How can you know if they take delight in the tree?'

'And you are not me,' the master said. 'How can you know what I do and don't know?'

How to play hide and seek with your own awareness

First, your attention is *no where*.

Next, your attention is *now here*.

Play is repeated constantly and is seldom won, never completely lost, and no one is quite sure who started it.

How many Zen practitioners does it take to change a light bulb?

- One to change the light bulb
- One not to change the light bulb
- One to realise they are the light bulb

A former monk who was now a successful businessman returned to his teacher, a Zen abbot, and gave him all his money.

'What is this for?' the abbot asked.

'It is to show you my gratitude and to give you happiness,' the businessman replied.

On hearing this the abbot threw all the money into the fire.

'Why did you do that?' he asked.

'To show my gratitude to the fire and to give it happiness,' the abbot said.

IMPERMANENCE
IMPERMANENCE
IMPERMANENCE
IMPERMANENCE
IMPERMANENCE
IMPERMANENCE
IMPERMANENCE
IMPERMANENCE
IMPERMANENCE
IMPERMANENCE
IMPERMANENCE
IMPERMANENCE
IMPERMANENCE
IMPERMANENCE
IMPERMANENCE
IMPERMANENCE
IMPERMANENCE
IMPERMANENCE

Nothing happens next,

this is it!

A conversation between two Zen monks:

> 'What did your face look like before you were conceived?'
>
> 'I did not have a face.'
>
> 'Who was this "I" who did not have one?'
>
> 'He was "I" without a face.'
>
> 'Then what did this "I" look like? What name did it answer to?'
>
> 'I was yet unseen, and without ears for a name.'
>
> 'Are you still he?'
>
> 'Only if you don't look.'

To see the true nature of any thing,

look beyond its name.

Land for sale

One square metre. Includes Bodhi tree. Suit monk.

The river speaks a love letter,

written in the rain,

carried by the mountain,

longing for the sea.

Zen Master:

'If you have a bowl, I will give one to you.

If you do not have a bowl, I will take it from you.'

Zen has no idea.

Study it diligently.

One way to completely wreck a moment

is to let it remind you of some other time.

Past love: just memories

Future love: just fantasies

True love: just now

MULTIPLE CHOICE ZEN

What is the difference between a duck?

a one leg is the same

b two minus one ducks

c I compare everything only with itself

d pass the orange sauce

Throw a stone in the pond,

gold or granite,

splash!

CRITICAL ZEN

'I wish you'd be a bit more thoughtless!'

MANY HAPPY RETURNS

Two Zen masters met for a walk. It was the birthday of one master. They were great friends.

'There is a gift for you under that tree.'

'I find nothing here.'

'Ah, good! It's still there then.'

'This gift is thoughtless and meaningless.'

'Don't mention it, it was nothing.'

They walked on together, laughing softly and pointing at birds.

DIARY OF A ZEN MAN

Morning:

3:00 a.m.   Chased the dog with no legs.

5:00 a.m.   Found an upside-down circle.

7:00 a.m.   Made the sound of one hand clapping.

9:00 a.m.   Put the boulder in the thimble.

11:00 a.m.   Met the Buddha on the path.

Lunch

To wish for the same dream to return

leaves no room for another.

A scorpion and a fox met at the river bank. The scorpion asked the fox, 'Will you carry me on your back across the river? I cannot swim.'

The fox replied, 'No, you're a scorpion, and you will sting me!'

'Why would I sting you? We would both drown!' the scorpion said.

After thinking about this, the fox invited the scorpion to sit on his back and he began to swim. In the middle of the river the scorpion raised his tail and plunged his stinger into the fox. As they were drowning the fox cried out, 'Why did you do that?'

'It's my nature,' the scorpion replied.

Normal is an opinion.

I will point to where

you can see the moon,

but to see it you need

to stop looking at my finger.

A DISCOURSE ON EMPTINESS

The following page is potently Zen.

Avoid thought when you see it.

Try to *see* without *looking*.

Alternatively, don't even look at it.

The teacher held up a wooden bowl and asked, 'What is this?'

'A bowl,' the student replied.

The teacher threw the bowl to the student. 'Bowl is a word. Is the thing in your hands a word?'

The word 'water' rarely sates a thirst.

SPORTS FOR THE ZEN-MINDED

Zenball: throw the ball without it leaving the hand.

(Hours of fun!)

QUIET AS A MOUSE

Four monks gathered together to meditate in silence for a month. On the first day a mouse ran across the floor of the dojo. The first monk exclaimed, 'There's a mouse!'

'Aren't we supposed to remain silent?' the second monk asked.

'Could you two please be quiet?' the third monk said.

'Ha, ha!' the fourth monk said as he leapt up triumphantly. 'I am the only one who did not speak.'

Less like and dislike;

more light and delight.

THE UNKNOWN TEACHER

A venerable Zen master lived alone in a little hut in the mountains. One day an unknown monk came to visit him. 'Welcome, Monk,' the master said. 'I am just now leaving to work in the field. Please cook anything you like for lunch, only bring me a little too.' ⟶ When the master returned that night he was very hungry because the stranger had not brought him his lunch. But he discovered that the monk had cooked himself a glorious meal, thrown away all the remaining food, and was now sleeping peacefully on his bed. When the master himself lay down to sleep, the monk got up and left forever. ⟶ Years later the master told this story to some students and said, 'He was such a good monk! I miss him still.'

MEDITATION

Don't just do something, sit there.

A MEDITATION

I probably should go shopping. My knee is sore. Did I post that bill? I wonder if I'm doing this right? … follow the breath in and out … ah, softness… breathe, here… in… out …

BUDDHIST LIBRARY

NOBLE SILENCE PLEASE

Be very, very quiet and you may hear the sound of nothingness.

Asserting what is true Zen is like arguing about where the tiger lives while it's eating you.

Zen in a nutshell

Maybe things aren't what they seem to be, but they're probably not something else either.

A Zen master lay dying on his bed. In attendance, were all the monks of the order. The eldest of the monks leant over the master and softly asked for any last words of wisdom for him to give to the gathered monks.

'Tell them wisdom is like a river,' the master said. The eldest monk repeated his words.

A young monk in the group asked, 'What does he mean by saying, "Wisdom is like a river?"'

The elder monk softly conveyed the young monk's question to the master.

'Okay, wisdom is not like a river,' the master replied.

This moment is your life time.

THE PAINTING LESSON

'Paint a circle with your brush,' the Zen Master instructed his student. The student dipped her brush in the ink and made a stroke. 'Good,' said the master. 'Now paint a circle with no mind to do so.' ⟶ The student sat before her paper unable to move for the rest of the lesson. As the years passed, she began to carry her paper with her everywhere, painting circles unceasingly with a heart to create one that was pure. ⟶ After ten years the student awoke one morning and knew that the time had come. She went to the master and said, 'I have come to thank you for my painting lesson. Would you like to see me paint the circle?' ⟶ The master looked at the student and said, 'There is no need for paper and brushes. I can see already what you have learnt and it is beautiful beyond compare.'

ZEN ART

Beyond technique,

without critique,

pure of heart,

artless art.

The most reassuring thing about Zen

is its lack of answers.

For nearly every why,

you'll find a why not.

Baby Bodhidharma

(China or bust.)

ATTENTION

You just took a breath without thinking about doing so. You probably just took another breath while thinking about doing so.

Zen is the practice of immediate experience, which is the bit left over when your mind isn't busy somewhere else.

One day a student of Zen went to the master and asked, 'Master, where do you learn all the wisdoms of the stories you tell us.' ⟶ The master replied, 'One day a student went to the master and asked, "Master, where do you learn…"'

The river Zen has no rocks to cling to.

DON'T GIVE IT ANOTHER THOUGHT

A powerful action is one performed when the mind and body accord without a second thought, acting wholly within the moment. This is where genius, wisdom and sincerity live, but they are constantly changing their address.

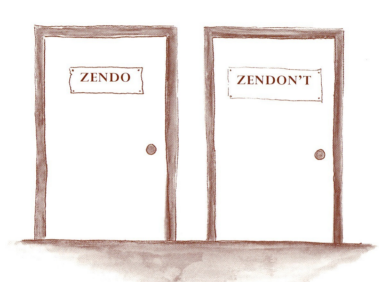

NOW AND ZEN

Only with attachment to outcome is there hesitancy.

Note: When crossing the road attachment to outcome is healthy.

Two monks came to a river and there they met a woman in a beautiful silk dress. The woman was worried about how to cross the river without ruining her dress. The elder of the two monks let her climb onto his back and carried her across the river. ⬩ After they waved goodbye to the woman, the monks walked on for several hours until, eventually, the younger monk could not keep silent any longer. He asked the elder monk, 'What were you thinking by carrying that woman across the river when you have taken a vow never to have physical contact with the opposite sex?' ⬩ The old monk looked surprised for a moment and said, 'It is true, earlier today I carried a woman across the river. I carried her for only two minutes. You have been carrying her for several hours.'

Good Zen action: If you see a weed, you pick it.

Not good Zen action: If you see a weed, you think, 'There's a weed, I should pick it,' and then you pick it.

Zen-less action: You don't see the weed despite it being next to you.

Zen-like inaction: You realise that the only difference between the weed and a flower is your thoughts on the matter.

Action void of Zen: To have considered all of the above with deliberation instead of just picking the weed.

Good Zen action: If you see a weed, you pick it.

PRESENT MOMENT PRESS
ZEN NEWS
SOMETHING TO WRAP YOUR FISH IN

No-thing remains elusive!
Reports in suggest that no-thing has still not materialised, suggesting it is truly *mu*. When asked for an opinion the Master said, 'no-thing matters.'

Mime artist injured
A mime was believed to be injured when a tree fell in the woods today. No one was there, nor heard anything; but unconfirmed reports suggest that it may or may not have happened.

Monk to sit down
A monk, who prefers to remain nameless, has vowed to sit in meditation until nothing in particular happens. He says he would like to achieve absolutely nothing at all within an indefinite time-frame, and gain no merit whatsoever.

Positions become vacant
The monastery is still looking for a new cook, since the last one kicked a bucket and got promoted to Abbot. To further complicate matters, the new Abbot has now left to pursue a career in quantum physics. Applicants wanting to replace the Abbot should be ego-free and, therefore, shouldn't apply. All enquires should not be directed to anyone by the end of the week.

Tao daily
The One that can be written about is not the true One. Confucius said nothing today.

Lecture postponed
The recently advertised lecture on 'the nature of impermanence' has been postponed following the unfortunate demise of the guest speaker. His last words are reported to have been, 'I told you so.'

Everything not you is *that*.

You are *that* too.

Be nice to *that*.

Compassion

Passion

Passion

I

THE BEST QUESTION TO ASK

A Zen abbot grew tired of one monk's endless questions.

'You may ask me any one question, but only one, and I promise to give you the true answer,' he said.

After hours of deliberation the student exclaimed, 'Master, what is the best question to ask?'

'That is,' replied the abbot. 'And that is your true answer.'

You are the living manifestation

of a rhetorical question.

Compare everything, but only to itself.

There is only one thing.

Everything is a very good explanation of that.

Those who speak about it, tend not to know about it.

Those who know about it, tend not to speak about it.

Those who are in the latter category are very annoying.

The tree has no intention to make a reflection.

The water has no mind to give it one.

A student went to a great Zen teacher and asked, 'Great Teacher, what is the afterlife like?'

The teacher replied, 'How could I possibly tell you. I have never died in my life.'

Take care of **now**, one now at a time,

and the rest of all time takes care of itself.

Knowledge speaks.

Wisdom listens.

Lunch tends not to do either,

and noon arrives regardless.

This sentence is not true.

Nor is this one.

ORIGINAL MIND

Think on the you that was,

before first you had a thought.

HELLO, IS THAT THE 'HOME DHARMA SHOPPING NETWORK'? IT'S ABOUT THE INSTANT KARMA YOU SENT ME...

I'm terribly sorry, I think my karma just ran over your dogma.

One day a venerable Zen master sat in a patch of sun by a well and began to meditate. After a time two monks came and joined the master, sharing the sun in their meditation. Several hours passed in silence, then one of the monks said, 'The well is deep.' ⟶ A further two hours passed and the second monk said, 'The well is not deep.' ⟶ After another two hours had passed the master stood up, saying, 'I came here to meditate, not to listen to you two argue!'

IDENTITY DARE

Be no one.

ULTIMATE ZEN

Realise who is reading this.

(No names, please.)

Your true nature is to be found

where you are standing right now.

That is the best place in the world

to find enlightenment.

The frog who lives at the bottom of the well

may truly believe he has seen the world.

If you make a fist,

then open your hand,

where is the fist?

100% ZEN LIFE

When you are making a cup of tea,

be mindful *only* of making a cup of tea.

(The application of this principle is especially useful when you are negotiating four-lane highways or fighting tigers.)

'Original mind' is a state of pure conception before preconception. Sort of like this sentence before it had words in it.

Thoughts are like rain drops on water.

Let them wash you to the sea.

DID YOU KNOW THAT YOU ARE THE REPRESENTATIVE OF AN ASPECT OF UNIVERSAL KNOWLEDGE?

A tiny leaf may fill your being with thought,

while a universe revolves unnoticed.

Neither is less nor more.

THE SECRET OF HAPPINESS

Have no preference.

It is the empty space

inside the bowl

that is useful.

A renowned Zen master lived a simple life in a small hut high in the mountains. One night a thief came to rob him, only to find the master had nothing of value. ⟶ On discovering the thief in his home the master gave the thief his clothing; not wanting the thief to have come so far for nothing. ⟶ After the thief had left confused, the master sat naked looking at the moon. 'Poor man,' he said, 'If only I could have given him this beautiful moon.'

Few things are as simple as peace.